THE PATRIARCHS

A WORKBOOK FOR INDIVIDUALS AND SMALL GROUPS

Named: The Patriarchs contributors include Annie Carter, Merritt Nielson, Richard Buckner, and Joseph Bentz.

Scripture quotations marked NIV are from *The Holy Bible, New International Version®* (NIV®). Copyright © 1973, 1978, 1984, 2011 by Biblica, Inc.™ Used by permission. All rights reserved worldwide.

10 9 8 7 6 5 4 3 2

CONTENTS

INTRODUCTION

Noah, The Woman at the Well, Thomas, Hagar; these men and women are more than just names in Bible stories. They were flesh and blood people. And in seeing how God moved in their lives, we can see him moving in ours. We can hear him call us by name.

Named is a 6-week small group resource that tells the story of people from scripture through a new lens—exploring the mystery of faith with a literary touch. Each series introduces 6 different people from the Bible, unpacking one person's story every week.

This workbook has original stories that are accompanied by historical context for the characters and the times they lived in, insight into how they fit into God's story, and discussion questions to help participants see how God's story works in them. This is a unique opportunity for your group to engage the Scriptures both personally, and as a community. Through the power of history-based stories, you'll see the truth of how God works. Not just in ancient times and in other people, but how he works today and in us all. Become acquainted with the people identified by God in a story as particular as yours.

HOW TO GET THE MOST OUT OF THIS STUDY

In this workbook you will find 6 narrative stories about some of the Patriarchs of the nation of Israel. The Patriarchs were flawed, but willing men God used to form the heritage of our faith. They walked with God to overcome opposition, become champions of justice, and challenge the cultural norms.

The narratives are written to help you to begin to think about how these individuals might have been feeling or what they might have been thinking during their story. Each week before you get together with your group, you might want to read the scriptures that the narrative is based on so that you have a full picture of the story. As you work through the reading and journaling in this book, continue to think about the pieces of the stories that find themselves in your life. What can you learn from these stories and apply in your own life?

WHAT YOU'LL FIND IN EACH CHAPTER

CONTEXT

This section will give readers an understanding of what was going on around the person at the time of the story. Historical, societal, and religious background are given to help readers put themselves in the shoes of those whose stories they are about to read.

STORY

The narratives told in this study attempt to get inside the heads of those whose stories we may have heard hundreds of times before. The writers of these pieces have attempted, through research and reflection, to give us a brief glimpse into what these people might have been thinking and how they might have felt. As you read or listen to the story each week look for places where you can relate to the story—God's story.

PLACE IN GOD'S STORY

This section will give you a short description of how God's story found its place in this individual.

THE STORY FINDS ITS PLACE IN ME

These questions are designed to help you reflect on what you've read in order to find yourself in God's narrative. There is plenty of space available for journaling.

WRITERS

Annie Carter grew up in Oklahoma with her parents and two older sisters. She holds a BS in Communications and Creative Writing from Olivet Nazarene University in Kankakee, Illinois. Annie has been a student at The Writers Studio in New York since April of 2012. She currently lives in New York City with her cat, Olive.

Richard E. Buckner is the ministry product line editor of Beacon Hill Press of Kansas City. He has held this position for eight years, prior to which he served as the book coordinator and copy editor for Beacon Hill. Richard holds a BA and an MA in religion from Southern Nazarene University and an MDiv from Nazarene Theological Seminary, where he served as reader for the professor of Christian history and graduated summa cum laude.

Merritt Neilson Merritt Nielson is the director of curriculum for the Church of the Nazarene. He has served as media producer, pastor, missionary, university professor and administrator, and social-service agency director. He is the creator of the popular *Ashes to Fire* series published by Beacon Hill Press. Nielson received his doctor of ministry from Gordon-Conwell Theological Seminary in vocation formation. He and wife Linda have four children and three grandchildren.

Joseph Bentz's books span a variety of genres, including a fantasy novel, three contemporary novels, and four nonfiction books on Christian living. His most recent release is *Pieces of Heaven: Recognizing the Presence of God.* Bentz is a professor of English at Azusa Pacific University in Southern California. He lives with his wife and two children in Southern California. His blog, Life of the Mind and Soul, appears at his website, www.josephbentz. com.

NOAH

THE WAITING • KEY SCRIPTURE PASSAGE: Genesis 6—8

HIS CONTEXT

The name *Noah* means "rest." It must have been no accident that the man most associated with tumultuous circumstances is called by name to be a source of rest. When we meet Noah, we find that wickedness had become a way of life on earth—so much so that we are told God looked at humankind and was sorry He had made them. It is safe to say that, at this time, there was no rest for humanity. This is a far cry from the images we often associate with Noah of a jolly bearded man on a boat with two happy penguins. God himself was repenting that He had made humans, and in His wisdom He knew it was time to do away with what had become of life in the world. The earth itself was now going to have a rest from wickedness, and God had identified Noah as the key player in His plan.

In the midst of the chaos, God saw Noah and "Noah found grace in the eyes of the Lord." Noah's story becomes inextricably tied up in this one sentiment. His story is marked by grace. Not only does God preserve Noah's own life, but He extends His grace to Noah by allowing his family, his sons and their wives, to be saved as well. Included in God's plan is instruction to take on the boat plants and animals. This act in and of itself was a promise of sorts that there would be life after the flood. The storm would come, but it would also pass. And when it passed, God's plan would not abandon the family to an uncertain fate.

HIS STORY

In that uppermost attic room of the ship the air was very still and full of dust.
The old man was in front of the window with his linen shirting open wide to cool
himself. The room was filled with the sounds of chirping and cooing and a cacoph-
ony of bird life from the rows of raffia cages hanging all around. The old man had
always liked the bird room best. He closed his eyes and swayed and shuffled
across the floor in his bare feet, and he smiled and clapped to their music.

When he opened his eyes, the dove watched from the edge of the table. Noah
was suddenly dizzy and reached out to steady himself. Although the boat had
been still for months, he was occasionally overcome with a sense of motion as if
they were all still trapped in the rocking back and forth. He sat heavily into a bench
beside the table and rested. Other than the bird, the only other object on the table
was a small branch Noah had weighted down with a wrapped loaf of bread. He
took the twig now and tucked it behind his ear, and this made him smile although
he was not sure why.

After some time, Noah took a wedge of the barley bread from its oilcloth and
broke it in two. The crumbs fell across the tabletop and Noah scooped them
into a little pile for the bird. The dove danced around the crumbs a moment but
instead sidled away and lighted on what was left of the loaf. It set to tearing at the
bread, pulling it apart piece by piece. Noah turned away. He took up a clay cup of
water from the windowsill and lifted it to drink, but he saw the water sway inside
the rim of the cup and he winced. He set it back on the ledge and waited for the
water to calm. In a cup it looked quiet and clear. The thought came to him that
he would never drink water again if he were to have a choice. He picked up the
cup and turned it over and water spilled out over the table and ran over the edges
across his lap and onto the floor. The dove looked up from where it had mangled

the bread. Noah took the little branch from behind his ear and drew it through the water like a paintbrush.

The old man's concentration was broken by shadows and noise outside the window. He stood and leaned out into the air. The warmth of the outdoors was still damp and heavy with the receding water. Noah squinted to see his son Ham bent over the dead body of a lamb. The ship was growing short on provisions, and it had taken some considerable debate with the family to come to a consensus on the necessity of a sacrifice. Noah had explained that his word counted twice, once for himself and once for the Almighty, and the matter had been settled.

Ham had hung the lamb from the doorframe of the boat to drain its blood into a large bowl and then carried the body into the daylight to remove its hide. He was bent at his work and now straightened up and wiped his forehead and mouth with the back of his hand. His shirt was tied by the sleeves around his hips. His shoulders and arms shone with sweat. The blade hung relaxed in the grip of his right hand and blood ran from the hilt into the sand.

Ham kept pacing the ground left to right and shifting his feet to keep from sinking in the mud up to his ankles. He turned his back to the sun and walked to the sodden ship sunk deep in the mud below Noah. There had been little left on the boat that was not damp to its core, so Ham had pulled planks of pine and pallets of hay from his own bed to stack in as organized a fashion as he could manage for the altar. Noah looked down at the meager thing and sighed. His son reappeared carrying a flint stone and a basin of oil. Ham lifted the prepared carcass of the lamb and laid it across the wood. A loose board gave way and a corner of the altar dropped out and the lamb slid to the mud nose first. Ham turned to look up at his father at the window, and Noah could see a streak of blood painted across his son's forehead where he had wiped his brow. Noah raised a hand to wave but Ham looked away, passing the blade from one hand to the other.

Noah looked down at the bird. He knew it was only fair to send it out again while it was still light. He was finding it hard to stomach the idea of letting it go again. Somehow he imagined this time might be the last time. He feared wasting any living thing. The old man leaned over the bird and whispered a blessing and implored it to be safe. With tears in his eyes he took the dove in his hand and lifted his arm out the window and into the open air, but the height suddenly seemed extraordinary and he drew is hands into the boat and held the white bird to his cheek and cried. The branch was still lying there and Noah took it in his hand and twirled it back and forth between his fingers. He broke off a piece and went back to the window and threw it out into the air. He watched it falling and thought of it there in the soil being warmed by the sun. With any luck the olive branch would grow and Noah would have done his part to till the earth back to life.

❝The old man leaned over the bird and whispered a blessing and implored it to be safe.❞

He was still watching the thing fall when he felt the presence of the bird. It had lighted on the windowsill and was at his left elbow. They had both been watching the branch fall. Noah reached out and touched the plume on the bird's head and then he raised his hand and felt the shine of his own bald head. A halo of gray hair still clung around his temples, and he tousled it and winked at the stout bird. It hopped twice and jumped to his right hand and he lifted it up to see it better. They considered each other for a moment, eyes turning this way and that. Noah found himself apologizing to the dove. Somewhere far away something was growing and there was life and Noah had to believe that they would find it. He thanked the dove and apologized again. Then he leaned out the window a last time and tossed the bird into the air and it was gone in a flash of white wing almost as soon as it had caught the wind. His son, observing all of this, took a step away and called out to his father that he would go into the boat and bring back fire.   —AC

NOAH

▼

13

"Somewhere far away something was growing and there was life and Noah had to believe that they would find it.**"**

HIS PLACE IN GOD'S STORY

It would be fair to assume that rest may not have always come easily during the turmoil of Noah's life story. The eccentricities of a man who would build a boat on dry land must have plagued his social experiences. He would have spent much of his life being ridiculed, not to mention the tremendous amount of waiting that punctuated Noah's story. He dedicated years to building an ark and then was called to enter the boat with his family a week before the rains began. Then the rains fell for 40 days and nights, and we are told that water covered the earth for something around 150 days. Next, the water had to recede, the ground had to dry up, and then the earth was tested for livability several times by sending out birds to find land.

In the midst of all of this waiting, Noah had to rely on an extraordinary faith to assure him that he was not waiting in vain and that he had not been abandoned there floating on the raging waters, but that there was in fact a plan in place, however vague it may have felt at times. Such is our heritage. Noah is called one of the fathers of faith. Faith being "the certainty that what we hope for is waiting for us, even when we cannot see" the dry land for miles.

While the lives of Noah and his family were saved by grace and sustained by faith, they were still men and women who had witnessed the wickedness that had previously pervaded the earth. They had also now lived through waters from heaven crashing down on them and water from the depths of the earth bursting forth and traversing on an entire world covered in water as the only raft of life anywhere. These were not weak and trembling men and women. And if they had been, they certainly weren't once the ark's door was opened again. They had survived trauma and would never forget it.

A recurring theme we see crop up time and again in the Old and New Testaments is the idea that there is no vessel too broken to be used by God. Stubborn Jonah, Rahab the prostitute, Paul the killer of Christians, and Jesus, a baby born in a livestock stable. Included in this list with many others would also be Noah. As we follow his life after the flood, we find a man who had his own share of brokenness. The Scriptures tell about the problems for his family that resulted one time when he drank too much wine. God knew that Noah had his flaws, and yet He chose him. Despite Noah's imperfections, he had enough insight to walk off the boat and immediately worship and sacrifice to the God of his salvation. And it is within Noah's story that we are told God acknowledges that "man's bent is always toward evil, [but] as long as the earth remains, there will be springtime and harvest, day and night." And we are promised rest once again and assured that there is a story in place and a plan for when the waters recede.

THE STORY FINDS ITS PLACE IN ME

1. What parts of Noah's story find their place in you?

2. In the context of your daily life, where are the areas you can see a need to let go and rest your faith in God's ability to complete the story?

3. It is important to reflect with due praise on the times in our life that are defined by grace. Take a moment to meditate on the times in your life when you can see the evidence of a miraculous plan at work.

4. In what ways has God asked you to wait as Noah and his family did? Are you still waiting?

5. How do you remain faithful in times of waiting on the Lord?

NOTES

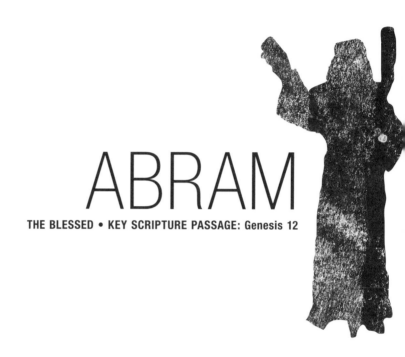

ABRAM

THE BLESSED • KEY SCRIPTURE PASSAGE: Genesis 12

HIS CONTEXT

Abram (ca. 2000 BC) was a seminomad, a pilgrim and occasional farmer, living in a goat-hair tent lit by an olive oil lamp. But he was not poor. He had many possessions ranging from livestock to slaves. He belonged to a tribal culture and was the head of a family within his father's clan, a subgroup within a tribe. Surrounding him were the advanced civilizations of Mesopotamia and Egypt, whose existence encouraged clear roads for travel.

Family, immediate and extended, was priceless to Abram's culture. Like the parts of a body, family members were bound to each other and the family group. Severing anyone from the family was like cutting off an arm or a leg; it was painful and often unbearable. Deciding to leave his father's family and relatives was an act of exceptional surrender for Abram. But his choice reflects his concern for the greater group, which in the blessings of Genesis 12:1-3 encompassed the families of the world.

Living in a polytheistic culture, Abram's decision was also a choice to follow one God among many. Unlike his family, who worshipped different gods (Joshua 24:2), Abram narrowed his trust to this one God. Here again Abram steps beyond the common practice of his culture.

That Abram and Sarai were barren was a grave matter. Barrenness was considered a curse and reproach for a couple, especially the woman. Children were a blessing, a sign of divine favor, and a son was a blessing of the highest order. Boys added to the clan when they married, joining to it their wives and children. Girls only decreased the clan, becoming members of their husband's family. Abram must ponder his situation and advancing age, as well as Sarai's, when hearing the blessing about being a great nation. Such a prospect would entail the birth of a male child and that again means placing trust in this God.

Light was important to tent dwellers like Abram. Olive oil fueled the lamps that dispersed the shadows of night. For travelers arriving after dark at a tent encampment, these lamps, which remained lit all night long, were signs of life. Only the poorest of tent dwellers lacked oil for lamps. Like a lamp lit in a dark tent or a star at dusk, the Voice calling Abram's name was a sign of life bursting into the barren darkness encompassing both Abram and humanity.

HIS STORY

A single light pierced the encroaching darkness, as the first star appeared in the dusky sky. Slowly the deepening shadows of night were kept at bay as more bright specks blinked into view.

Abram reclined outside his tent, gazing upward and enjoying the evening breeze. The day had been dry and hot, and he welcomed the soothing wisps of air against his face. The coolness helped him relax and eased his mood so he could sort through the thoughts swirling in his head. Right now he was thinking about this morning. About the . . . he could hardly form the words in his own mind he was so incredulous . . . *the Voice.* He could not stop thinking about it.

It happened just before dawn. He had barely stepped through the opening of his tent when he heard his name: "Abram." He peeked back inside, to the curtained quarters of his wife, Sarai, thinking she might have roused and called to him. But all he heard was her slumbered breathing. As he started to turn, he heard it again: "Abram." The Voice was firm but gentle. He couldn't tell which direction it was coming from. He stepped farther from the tent and looked around, "Yes? I hear you. Where are you?"

A conversation then ensued that was more astonishing than any Abram had ever had. A conversation with a Someone that he never saw but whose presence seemed more real than the ground on which he stood. A conversation with a Voice that seemed to come from everywhere and nowhere all at the same time. All day he had mulled over what this Voice had asked him to do. He also thought about the incredible promises the Voice had made. And now as night was falling, Abram was musing over what all this meant to everyone and everything in his life.

He thought about his family and recalled the long journey he had made when his father, Terah, set out to move their entire household to Canaan. After months of travel, when they had arrived just north of Canaan, he decided to stop. So Abram, Sarai, and Abram's nephew Lot and all their possessions settled with Terah in Harran.

> **"'I will make . . . ,' 'I will bless . . . ,' and 'I will curse . . .' The words buzzed over and over again in Abram's ears. Who could do all the Voice said it would do? Who?"**

And now this curious Voice had just asked him—in fact told him—to do something that made no sense at all. "Go," the Voice had said. "Leave the land in which you've settled and your father's household, and travel to a land I will show you." Leaving Harran was no problem; after all, Abram was used to moving from place to place. Hadn't his entire clan traveled the long distance from Ur? But to leave all his relatives, except for his immediate family, that was another matter. His family was priceless. Dividing a clan was like cutting a person in half; the pain was unbearable.

Abram shook his head. Perhaps there had been no Voice at all . . . perhaps in his early morning drowsiness his imagination had gotten the better of him.

But the Voice had made a promise, and an incredible promise at that. If he did as the Voice said, Abram was to receive honors and riches beyond any of his dreams. They were the kinds of privileges only a monarch could hope to enjoy. Could it even be possible? What would people say? Abram, the father of a great nation? Everyone knew Sarai was barren. But the Voice had talked about a people who would come out of Abram's own loins, a great people having their own language, land, and government. And then came the list of blessings.

Abram noticed immediately that the blessings the Voice promised increased in greatness from one to the next. Carefully, Abram recalled each, reflecting on its meaning. First was the blessing Abram would receive personally. He individually would be the recipient of great favor. His name would then be made great, which along with becoming a great nation was an honor worthy of a king. Abram and his name would be so great that he himself would be a blessing. People would use his name and say, "May God make me as blessed as Abram." A smile tugged at his lips as he remembered the wonder of those words.

Not only would Abram be blessed and his name employed in blessing, but the Voice told him even those persons who were kind to him would live in favor. The Voice then added that curses would come to those who even so much as insulted him. He couldn't imagine it. Blessings or curses for those who blessed or defamed Abram. This was a promise of protection of the highest order! Finally, the Voice announced to Abram that all the clans of the world born through Abram would receive blessing as well.

"I will make . . . ," "I will bless . . . ," and "I will curse . . ." The words buzzed over and over again in Abram's ears. Who could do all the Voice said it would do? Who?

"Could this be El Shaddai . . . the Almighty? Something deep within Abram stirred, a feeling he had never known before.**"**

The only One who could make and keep such promises would have to be the God who Abram had heard about in his childhood. Surely this was the same One he had learned about at the knees of his parents. Surely the Voice could only belong to El Shaddai, the Almighty One who had once caused a great flood over all the earth and who had stirred up such a commotion at a place called Babel that people scattered in all directions.

Could this be El Shaddai . . . the Almighty? Something deep within Abram stirred, a feeling he had never known before.

He stood and stretched. The night was growing long. He wasn't sure how the Voice would fulfill all those promises. He and Sarai were growing old, and time was running out for her. How could he become a great nation? The land to where he would be going was another matter. There were probably all kinds of people living there. If that was so, Abram didn't see how he was going to lay claim to it. And then there was the pain of parting from his clan. Would his family ties be broken forever?

Yet Abram could not forget the Voice. If he closed his eyes, he could still feel it compelling him, calling to a place deep within his own spirit. He could hear the intimate way it had said his name: "Abram." For an instant, even at the memory of it, he lost his breath. El Shaddai?

Abram brushed the dust off his robe and turned toward his tent. All was dark inside, except for the oil lamp Sarai had lit. It was a single bright spot amid the blackness. Abram made his way through the door. He paused to pick up the lamp and carried it to the curtained area where Sarai slept. As he parted the goat-hair partition, the light from the lamp fell across her face. For a moment he watched her sleep. "Sarai. Sarai . . ."   —RB

HIS PLACE IN GOD'S STORY

Abram's encounter with God (Genesis 12:1-3) marks a turning point in God's story. Until then, the story consisted of several cycles made up of human disobedience and divine judgment tempered by grace. From the fall in Eden to the flood and the tower of Babel, the divine-human drama was a bleak affair. By the time of Abram, the tragedy had reached a point so low that the mention of Sarai's barrenness echoed that of humanity's (11:30). Humankind had devolved to the unfruitfulness of a sterile womb.

Into this dark futility, God spoke to Abram, and, like a star at dusk, broke through the gloom. God's call and Abram's response was a defining moment for God's relationship with humankind. God's attention would from then on be on Abram and his family as agents of God's new and marvelous plan to restore humankind to what it was meant to be. Though the culmination of this plan would come many centuries later, God's opening address to Abram was the crucial beginning.

Into the life of this seminomad, God spoke blessings and promises, all hinging on Abram's trust and obedience. With the first promise to Abram, that he would be a great nation, God dispelled the barrenness in Abram's life. Then in the successive blessings God promised to dispel the barrenness in the lives of others through Abram. The final promise—that in Abram a blessing would come to all the families of earth—was the culminating word that humanity's dark times would finally be over.

In the years following this first meeting, God would repeat and clarify his promises to Abram and ensure them with covenantal ritual. But none of this would happen without Abram's costly decision not only to give up the nearness of his extended family but also to stake his life and future on this curious God who called him by name. By making his choice Abram opened the way for God to work in the lives of his descendants. Through these prophets, priests, kings, and everyday people would someday come One who would truly pierce the world's darkness. On a foreboding cross and later at a garden tomb, the brilliant climax of God's story would at last come into view.

THE STORY FINDS ITS PLACE IN ME

1. What part of Abram's story find its place in you?

2. Reflect on Abram's story. What are the possible consequences of disobedience? What are the benefits of obedience?

3. How do you know when God wants you to do something? How quickly do you respond?

4. Tell of a time when you obeyed God. What happened? Do the same for a time you disobeyed.

5. Think about your family and possessions. How willing would you be to give up any of them if God asked?

NOTES

JACOB

THE SURRENDERED • KEY SCRIPTURE PASSAGE: Genesis 32

HIS CONTEXT

God has plenty of time to refine character and prepare those who seek Him for the great challenges of life. It may take twenty, even forty years. God is not in a hurry. For those who diligently desire Him, who long to grasp the promises of grace, God provides ample time to develop the character that prepares and sustains the Jacobs of the world for the moments of their greatest challenges.

Pursuing those divinely inspired desires is worth everything. It is difficult to know what the deep motivations of Jacob's heart were. Yet we can imagine that something of the magnificence of the true and living God engaged Jacob's soul as a young boy in the tents of Isaac and Rebekah. Those stories—the oral traditions that passed on the life-events of his grandfather Abraham—were important to him. They ignited a passion to grasp the promises that this God had made with mortals—and in particular, a promise to his grandfather that untold blessing would cover the earth through his numerous-as-the-sands-of-the-sea descendants.

What does Jacob eventually learn? The blessings of God are not ours to get on our terms, but God's to give on God's terms.

HIS STORY

The lone figure looked pensively at the western horizon. The sun had disappeared quickly, and night had crept in from the east with a thin sliver of moon hanging in a sea of brilliant stars. A thick foreboding settled over the lonely ravine that led away from the Jabbok River. The man shivered. Was it simply the night air? He crouched low, pulling his shepherd's tunic around his strong bent legs. A pervasive loneliness ached in his heart.

This night was trouble. Jacob looked back across the Jabbok and saw the faint glow of fires in his encampment. He wondered if by tomorrow everything would be gone, including his family and livestock, all of it slaughtered by Esau. He could not help but think—about *everything*. As he rehearsed the events that had broken his relationship with his brother, he felt ashamed. What had ever possessed him to take for himself what was only God's to give?

"I guess I've lived up to my name," he mumbled. "I am nothing but a heel grasper."

Life was closing in on him. The bleakness of the ravine, the black sky, the eerie silence sent another shiver through his tired muscles. Esau had been the strongest in their youth, but years of herding sheep and living as a nomad had toughened Jacob. Still he was not prepared for this. Somewhere out there, Esau was waiting with four hundred men to confront him and settle the score. Sometime after sunrise the two would meet.

Jacob stirred the embers in the small fire. Had it really been twenty years? Only recently, he had learned of his mother's death. Isaac, his father, as far as he knew, was still living. Esau, he was sure, had amassed riches and prestige. In the meantime, Jacob himself had become wealthy working for his uncle Laban, who had been good to him. His flocks increased each year and he had fathered eleven children by his concubines and his two wives—Leah and Rachel.

He picked up a stick and began drawing in the dusty earth still illuminated by a waning fire.

"The concubines will be first in the line of approach to Esau," he figured aloud as he began to map out a diagram in the dirt. "Then Leah and her children, and then my beloved Rachel and Joseph. If Esau begins a slaughter of revenge, perhaps Rachel and Joseph will have time to escape."

"Deliver me, please, from the hand of Esau, for I am afraid of him. He may come and kill us all, the mothers with the children. Yet you have said, 'I will surely do you good.'"

He suddenly felt a presence but could see no one. He hunkered down warily, looking around. There was no noise, only the disconcerting sense that he was not alone. Perhaps Esau had sent someone to attack him while he was vulnerable. Yet how would Esau know he was there, outside the camp? Was someone watching him, even now? He deserved it, he told himself, this night of fear—a bowl of lentil stew from his culinary bag of tricks in exchange for Esau's birthright.

The chill of the night air was making it more and more difficult to keep warm. It looked like the fires in his encampment across the Jabbok had gone out. His own little fire had spent itself, leaving only glowing coals. He sat very still. Remorse continued to plague him. There had been still more deception in his past—more than he wanted to remember. He thought of his mother's scheming idea to steal the firstborn's blessing—something that rightfully belonged to Esau. In her defense, she was only trying to bring about what she believed the Lord had promised. Rebekah had repeated the story many times to him during his growing-up years, describing the difficult months of her pregnancy and how the Lord's messenger had told her that the older twin would serve the younger. Together, his mother and he had connived to accomplish that prophetic word.

"I agreed to it," he admitted to himself. "I wanted it as much as she did." He stood and poked at the fading embers restlessly. "Tomorrow I face my brother—my accuser. Surely I will die." He said the words aloud to the darkness and shrugged. ". . . so be it." For God himself had brought Jacob to this place, his homeland, perhaps for his day of reckoning. Only a few hours earlier he had prayed over the peace gift he would send to his brother: "O God of my fathers Abraham and Isaac, who said to me, 'Return to your country and to your kindred, and I will do you good' . . . O Lord, I am not worthy . . . Deliver me, please, from the hand of Esau, for I am afraid of him. He may come and kill us all, the mothers with the children. Yet you have said, 'I will surely do you good.'" Jacob rehearsed the prayer again, praying it softly out loud.

Again, he felt uneasy in his surroundings; perhaps it was time to go back to camp. He lifted his head. In that instant, there was an arm around his neck, a huge arm, and he found himself on the ground. He struggled against the magnificent force on top of him, but soon his assailant pinned his shoulder to the rocky soil. Jacob couldn't see his face but managed to wriggle free and take the advantage. Jacob was lean and sinewy himself and his arms were strong, but it took every bit of strength he had to prevent his assailant from pinning him again. Around and

JACOB

around the hard dusty earth they rolled, lunging and grunting and exchanging dominance, each seeking the advantage. The phantom wrestler never spoke; he simply kept Jacob off balance though he could not quite prevail against Jacob's determined struggle. Just before dawn, the man forced Jacob down hard on his hip, and with a cry of anguish Jacob knew he was beaten. With his hip out of joint, his leg was now totally useless. The pain was excruciating. And yet he clung to his opponent with a strength he had never known. "Let me go," the man said. He was out of breath. "It's almost daybreak."

"No." Jacob's voice was muffled in the folds of his opponent's robe. "I will not let you go, unless you bless me."

The man's voice, suddenly strong, echoed off the sides of the narrow valley. "You have a new name: *Israel*—'you have striven with God and with humans, and have prevailed.'"

"Who *are* you?"

But the Night Visitor was gone. Jacob pulled himself up from the ground. He was alive, and strangely free. Dawn was growing in the east. Today he would meet Esau and ask forgiveness. He wasn't afraid. He took a step and winced; his limp would be proof that last night was no mere dream. Gingerly, he started down the ravine toward the camp.

—MN

//'No.' Jacob's voice was
muffled in the folds
of his opponent's robe.
'I will not let you go,
unless you bless me.'**//**

HIS PLACE IN GOD'S STORY

Jacob was facing the crisis of his life. But God was in charge, not Jacob. When it comes to our own dealings with God, we may think we are taking the initiative. But here is what I am coming to believe about the journey of faith. We always find that God is way ahead of us. We think we have chosen the time and place, but God is there first, loving God that He is. God puts into our hearts those good desires that arouse our discontent and drive us to himself. In Jacob's case it took God twenty years to bring him to this point of surrender on the border of the Promised Land. The Lord is not in a hurry. But when the magnificent moment arrives, the transformation is complete. We have not chosen the moment, the moment chooses us. You can trust those great moments. In Jacob's case it is a transition from self-help, self-direction, to faith in God who cripples Jacob in order to bless him.

THE STORY FINDS ITS PLACE IN ME

1. What parts of Jacob's story find their place in you?

2. Can you imagine what Jacob might have been feeling on this night before he faced the brother he stole from, lied to, and betrayed? Reflect on a time when you have been faced with a moment like this where you had to own up to your actions.

3. Even though Jacob made a demand of God, saying, "I will not let you go until you bless me" do you think Jacob's heart was surrendered to God? Can you think of a time in your life where you were wrestling with your circumstances and finally came to a place of surrender to God?

4. Jacob immediately left his home after deceiving his father and brother. Though he eventually came back and God blessed him, he spent years away from home and the path his mother felt was his. Have you ever had a time where your choices took the course of your life off track for a time? What brought you back?

5. Read Genesis 33 to see what happens next between Jacob and Esau. Think of a time when you have been the recipient of forgiveness on this level. What did it mean to you?

NOTES

JOSEPH

THE DREAMER • KEY SCRIPTURE PASSAGES: Genesis 37—50

HIS CONTEXT

Joseph's story is significant in showing how he is transformed as an *individual,* but it also carries huge implications for Israel as a *people.* Biblical scholar W. Lee Humphreys explains that the story of Joseph "brings the ancestors of the tribes of Israel into Egypt, and looks forward to Egyptian bondage and beyond to deliverance. This narrative thus appears as an elaborate transition piece between the patriarchs and the exodus, two basic themes within the sacred story. . . . In the linking of these themes Israel is transformed from a family into a people and potential nation."[1]

Joseph himself is aware that his story is bigger than himself. By the time he reveals his identity to his brothers in Genesis 45:8, he has been instrumental not only in guiding Egypt through two years of what will become a seven-year famine, but his actions also will preserve the line of Abraham, Isaac, and Jacob. His life certainly had not gone as he had planned it, but now he clearly sees God's hand at work in placing him exactly where he needed to be. He tells his brothers, "So then, it was not you who sent me here, but God. He made me father to Pharaoh, lord of his entire household and ruler of all Egypt" (Genesis 45:8, NIV).

Although God had revealed his ultimate plan for Joseph's life in the famous dreams Joseph has at age seventeen, the painful events during the years that followed those dreams must have bewildered the young man. The dreams (Genesis 37) showed the brothers' sheaves of grain bowing down to Joseph's sheaf, and the sun, moon, and eleven stars bowing down to Joseph. But during the years that followed those dreams, it must have been hard for Joseph to continue to believe they would come true. Think of how tempted Joseph must have been to feel completely abandoned by God during these low points of his life:

- His jealous brothers plot to kill him, then throw him into a cistern instead, and finally sell him into slavery. They never expect to see him again (Genesis 37).

- The wife of Potiphar, whom Joseph serves faithfully in Egypt, falsely accuses Joseph of attempted rape, landing him in prison (Genesis 39).
- Stuck in prison, he correctly interprets the dreams of Pharaoh's baker and cupbearer, but the cupbearer, once he is free, forgets about Joseph, who continues to languish in jail (Genesis 40—41).

In spite of harsh circumstances, Joseph stays faithful to God, waiting for the dreams of his youth to be fulfilled. In God's own unpredictable, roundabout timing, He eventually uses Joseph in a crucial way to prosper the people of Israel.

HIS STORY

When I was a young man, I bragged about my dreams. They were grandiose dreams, but they came true. My brothers hated me because of them. They hated me so much that they threw me into a cistern and sold me into slavery. I understand their bitterness a little more now. Who wouldn't resent a favored son? It didn't justify their cruelty against me, but I get it.

I am reconciled to my brothers, but they still don't really know me. When they look at me today, they see power. Second only to Pharaoh, I am literally clothed in power, from my regal headdress to my fine robes and adornments and golden staff. Servants and palace dignitaries alike bow to me, jump at my whispered command, attend to my every desire. My brothers are still rough-hewn shepherds. Set me side by side with them, and no one would guess we are related.

I still have dreams, but I no longer brag about them—or even whisper them—to anyone. These are not prophetic dreams, like the ones when I was young. These are nightmares. Sometimes I wake up certain that I am still in prison. In the darkness I open my eyes and feel that I am trapped in my filthy, barren cell and may never get out. I sometimes order the lamps to be lit to prove that I am in my own house, not in Pharaoh's jail.

> **"The past is always with me. I know how flimsy power is. I know I can't put my trust in anything or anyone except the Almighty God."**

Even during my waking hours, I feel everything might be snatched away from me in an instant, the way it was when Potiphar's wife falsely accused me of rape. Sometimes I smell the foul odor of that prison, and I order incense to be burned to take it away. Sometimes I can still taste the dirt that I had to wipe out of my mouth on the day my brothers threw me into the pit. Sometimes I am engulfed by the rage that swept through me when I used to fantasize revenge on those who had harmed me.

The past is always with me. I know how flimsy power is. I know I can't put my trust in anything or anyone except the Almighty God.

Nothing ever gets resolved.

When my father Jacob died, and we carried his body across the dusty miles to bury him in the land of Canaan among his ancestors as he requested, I thought his burial sealed the final chapter of the story of the rift and reconciliation between me and my brothers. My father had lived long enough to know that I, the beloved son he thought was dead, not only lived, but ruled under Pharaoh in Egypt. He saw the relationship between me and my brothers restored. He saw me save them from the famine and make a way for them to live and thrive in this land. He could not have expected anything more from me, and neither could my brothers. Their own lives and those of their families were spared, and the nation that had been promised to Abraham had been preserved.

I was surprised, then, when my brothers asked to see me once we returned to Egypt after burying Jacob. They would not reveal the purpose of their visit. What could they possibly want? More land? Better land? More grain? My assistant warned me, "They sound worried about something. Suspicious. They will speak only to you, but I sense fear in them."

I agreed to see them. Not all of them came. They sent only three—Simeon, Judah, and Benjamin. They were rough-looking men, cleaned up for this dinner but with calloused hands and dirt around the fingernails nonetheless. They entered my sitting room as strangers, bowing, keeping their distance, speaking to me in the careful, distant tones of a servant to a master.

Though they were bewildered in the midst of the pomp of my mansion, I set a feast before my brothers. My table was lavished with honey cakes, meat, wine, pomegranates, grapes, and bread. I hoped the meal would coax them out of their formality, but they ate politely, glancing at one another occasionally to make sure they weren't overdoing it. How much more they would enjoy this food if they were feasting on it around their own table in Goshen.

When they had eaten all propriety allowed, I asked, "What do you have to say to me, brothers?"

Judah, who sat directly across the table from me, was the spokesman. Taking a deep breath, he leaned forward. "Joseph, before our father died, he told us to come to you to plead for forgiveness for the crime we committed against you. We come as your slaves. For the sake of our father, we beg you not to carry out revenge against us. We are servants of the God of your father."

Though the sweet taste of the meal was still with me, bile rose in my throat. "Haven't I already done what you're asking, brothers?" I looked at each one in turn. "Didn't I rescue you from the famine? Didn't I set you up in the land of Goshen, where you and your families live in peace and plenty?"

"You have shown all of us every kindness—while our father lived."

"You think I acted mercifully *only for my father's sake*? And now that he is gone I will exact my revenge?" I couldn't conceal my anger.

They stayed silent for several uncomfortable seconds. Judah said, "You are a powerful man, Joseph. You could wipe us out with a word. Life is not like that for us. We rely on mercy."

"And what do you think I rely on? Have I always been a ruler in Egypt? I was a *slave,* Judah. You have been able to come and go as you please your whole life. I have lived at the whim of someone else. I used my power to save you, and now you doubt me?"

Benjamin, who had scarcely spoken a word that evening, no doubt on orders from the others, reached his strong arms across the table and took my hands in his. Touching me broke protocol, and at first Judah leaned forward as if to restrain Benjamin. "We honor you, Joseph," said Benjamin. "We thank you for your rescue of our family. We come in humility."

Brotherhood is what I wanted, but I would have to settle for this.

I stood and paced the room. "Am I God, brothers? Are your deeds for me to punish? Do you think I understand any more than you do why God works the way He does? Over and over I have asked Him why I had these dreams . . . and why He abandoned me to slavery. And yet, look what He has done—you are here with me, and I hold your future in my hands! Today, God himself saves you and so fulfills His promise to Abraham and to our own father Jacob. Go in peace."

Judah and Simeon passed a look of relief between them. They had received the reassurance they came for. Benjamin let go of my hands and leaned back, his gaze still intent upon me. I knew he felt the loss between us. We were strangers. I would never talk and laugh with my brothers as they did among themselves. I would not walk the hills with them for an afternoon or tend the animals or sit by the fire and tell stories. The distance was too great. No amount of forgiveness could close it.

After my brothers left that night, I sat alone for a long time at my empty dining table, pondering the unfathomable ways of our God. —JB

"Am I God, brothers? Are your deeds for me to punish? Do you think I understand any more than you do why God works the way He does? Over and over I have asked Him why I had these dreams . . . and why He abandoned me to slavery.**"**

HIS PLACE IN GOD'S STORY

As biblical scholar Robert Alter puts it, Joseph's story shows him being transformed "from spoiled brat to mature and shrewd administrator." His first appearance on the scene is not promising. In Genesis 37 his first recorded act is to bring a "bad report"—or essentially to tattle—against his brothers. As he matures, however, Joseph eventually becomes a more admirable figure in the midst of hardship than he was in his younger days as his father's favorite.

Joseph is put in situations that would have caused many people to despair, but the Bible records that he *prospered* in those places. He is never content to lose himself in self-pity. He makes the best of whatever circumstance he is in, no matter how unfair, and lets God take care of the results. Eventually, his faithfulness pays off, and he emerges from prison to become Pharaoh's right-hand man.

Being a slave could have made Joseph bitter and resentful, but instead, he thrives: "The LORD was with Joseph, and he prospered, and he lived in the house of his Egyptian master. . . . Potiphar put him in charge of his household, and he entrusted to his care everything he owned" (Genesis 39:2, 4, NIV). When Joseph is later unfairly imprisoned, he might easily have taken out his frustration by moping or becoming violent, but instead, he accepts God's goodness in the midst of difficulty and does the best work he can: "But while Joseph was there in the prison, the LORD was with him; he showed him kindness and granted him favor in the eyes of the prison warden. So the warden put Joseph in charge of all those held in the prison, and he was made responsible for all that was done there" (Genesis 39:20-22, NIV).

Humanly speaking, if Joseph had chosen to feel sorry for himself or lose his faith in God's plan for him, he would have died a forgotten slave or prisoner. Instead, he worked with competence and determination as he *waited* on God to rescue not only him but also his undeserving brothers.

THE STORY FINDS ITS PLACE IN ME

1. What parts of Joseph's story find their place in you?

2. Joseph's story is an example of God working out his purposes in roundabout and unexpected ways. Scripture is full of such stories. Make a list of examples that come to mind. Can you think of examples from your own life in which God seemed to work in ways you never could have anticipated and that you could only understand in hindsight? What impact does that have on how you trust Him in your current circumstances?

3. There are plenty of times when Joseph could have despaired. Instead, he prospered. Can you think of times in your life when the present looked very bleak, but you later saw how God was at work the whole time in the midst of those tough circumstances?

4. What if Joseph had been unwilling to forgive and instead had insisted on the revenge his brothers deserved? How would his story have been different? What significance does that need for forgiveness have in your own life?

5. Joseph's story is about more than himself. It is about the survival of his people. In what ways as Christians are our own stories about more than ourselves? Why is it so easy to lose that larger perspective? If you think of your story as part of the bigger story God is writing, how does it change the way you live?

NOTES

MOSES

THE RELUCTANT • KEY SCRIPTURE PASSAGE: Exodus 13—14

HIS CONTEXT

The dramatic story of the parting of the Red Sea does not, of course, turn out well for Pharaoh's army. You can find the story in Exodus 15.

The question arises, if God intended to destroy this army and rid the Hebrews of Pharaoh for good, why did He choose this way to do it? He could have wiped them out in any number of much simpler ways before they even got close to the Hebrews—by natural disaster, by disease. Why do it in such an unusual way that scares the Hebrews and that gives Moses yet another crisis to deal with?

This story happens not long after Moses and his people already thought they were rid of Pharaoh. That process of getting freed from him was also long, complicated, and difficult. Exodus 7—12 describes the 10 plagues it took for Pharaoh to finally give the Israelites their freedom.

Perhaps part of the answer lies in Exodus 14:4, when the Lord tells Moses that he will harden Pharaoh's heart and pursue the army "that I may gain glory through Pharaoh and through all his force, and the Egyptians will know that I am the Lord."

Moses and his people were part of something much larger than themselves. Throughout their story, God keeps doing things the hard way. At the time of the parting of the Red Sea, they had taken a route toward the Promised Land that was not the most direct route, and they were camped at a place where Pharaoh's army could easily attack them. God had a purpose, but they didn't know until the last minute what it was. They didn't understand God's timing, purpose, or methods.

HIS STORY

I ripped back the curtain of my tent in a fury, nearly yanking it from its rod. Five or six small clusters of men stood inside, waiting for me, staring and gauging my mood. I didn't want to see any of them. But neither did I want them to witness my wrath—no need to start more gossip in the camp, which was already crawling with rumors. I kept my gaze forward, steadying my breath, and stepped toward the next curtain, which opened to my own room, an inner sanctum I had ordered built into my tent. A place to pray, I had told them. To think, to plan.

And to get away from all of you.

Not that I always felt that way about them. But today was different. Today they would blame me for the horror that was about to swoop down upon us.

Even in my chamber, I could still hear the murmuring voices outside. If only I had stone walls to shut out the whiners, the complainers, and the second-guessers. Before I had time to sit down or light a lamp, the curtain opened and the stooped, tired figure of Aaron stepped inside. Had it been anyone else, my temper would not have held. Only he had permission to interrupt me when I entered this room.

"Where have you been?" he whispered, coming close. "These men need to see you. They don't know how to control the panic in the camp. They're saying Pharaoh's army is on the march against us."

"It's true. I went out to see for myself."

"Chariots, they say. Hundreds of them! They say some of their soldiers and chariots are already visible on the ridge behind us. We don't stand a chance if—"

"Aaron. I know. I've spent the last two hours walking around out there. I saw the Egyptian soldiers on that ridge. I saw the chariots. They're coming."

The Egyptians could see us too, no doubt. They could look down and see our women and children and tents and animals, and it all must have looked like a big, disorganized mass and an easy target. They were setting up camp above us. They were in no hurry; we were sitting ducks.

"So, what now?" asked Aaron.

I could sense the men eavesdropping on the other side of the curtain. My dark little room was no hideaway. I felt trapped. "Let's take a walk," I said.

I pushed through the curtain, hurried past the waiting men, and headed out into the sunshine. Aaron quickly followed, bringing with him only the assistants who sometimes served as our bodyguards as we walked through the camps, to keep people at a distance so we wouldn't be bombarded with every imaginable kind of request or complaint.

I walked fast, and Aaron struggled to keep up. I had already issued orders for everyone to prepare to march, so all through the dusty camp we walked past clusters of people frantically packing and moving their animals. When we reached a point in the camp that allowed a good view of the ridge behind us, I edged away from a knot of our own people who were staring up there, and I pointed out the Egyptians to Aaron.

"They are ready to strike," I said.

"We need a plan," he said. "They will slaughter most of us and drag the rest back to Egypt."

"We *have* a plan. We're executing it now." I spoke with a confidence I didn't feel.

"It's not much of a plan," he said bluntly, turning to face me head on. "To prepare to march? Where? Into the sea? Into the wilderness? Straight toward their army? Face it . . . it's over for us."

I looked over his shoulder at the chariots on the ridge. Even from this distance I could tell there were hundreds of them. For an instant, I was a boy back in Egypt, watching out the courtyard window as the soldiers trained. In those pampered days in the Egyptian court, chariots for me were associated with sports, lazy afternoons, showing off. They were simply one more pleasure in a life of rides down the river with my friends in my pleasure boat, big meals at the palace, music in the smoky evenings. I had never fit in there, not really. I didn't fit in this camp either, where hostile young men now tried to push past my guards. I had always been too Hebrew for the Egyptians and too Egyptian for the Hebrews. The chariots that once meant pleasure and power now signified nothing but dread. And death. And blame.

Aaron was still facing me, talking desperately. I watched his mouth move, but I didn't hear what he was saying. We had only one option. It was time to flee. From my former people, and from Pharaoh.

Someone from the crowd yelled, "What have you done to us now, Moses? Weren't there enough graves in Egypt? Is that why you had to bring us out here to the desert to die?"

"Grab that man!" Aaron shouted. "He can't—"

"No, let him go," I said. We pushed through the gathering mob. "Let's go back and get ready for what's to come."

These people second-guessed every decision I made. I was well aware of their murmurings. Why hadn't I led them on the more traveled route to the Promised Land, the one used by caravans and armies? Why had I brought them here to this desert, where they would certainly be crushed by Pharaoh? I couldn't blame them for wondering. It's certainly not what I would have chosen; if I had my way, we wouldn't be here. Do they think it's *my* presence that inhabits the pillar of cloud by day and the pillar of fire by night?

Aaron was sweaty and still very rattled by the time we made it back to the tent. He ordered everyone out.

"Now what?" he demanded. "We're in an impossible situation."

I closed my eyes. This would not be easy. I opened them and met Aaron's gaze. "I have heard from the Lord."

He raised his eyebrows, waited. By now he was used to these kinds of surprises.

"Gather the people, and tell them this: 'Do not be afraid. Take your station and see the Lord's deliverance that He will do for you today, for as you see the Egyptians today, you shall not see them again for all time. The Lord shall do battle for you, and you shall keep still.'"

Aaron himself stood deathly still for several seconds after I spoke, and then finally he shook his head slowly, smiled a tiny smile, and said, "They're not going to like it."

"No. But tell them."

He sighed and turned toward the entrance of the tent.

"Aaron." He paused, holding the tent flap. "Tell them we will be marching to the East."

He turned toward me, his face incredulous. "But that is toward . . ."

I interrupted him. "Tell them."

———————

Aaron made the announcement to the people, who had no choice but to continue with their preparations to move. The faces of the men betrayed their resignation . . . our situation was hopeless. As they worked through the afternoon, an east wind picked up, gusty at first but strengthening with every passing hour. The air began to thicken, and the pillar of cloud we followed slowly shifted to the west. I could no longer see the Egyptian chariots up on the ridge. The cloud spread out and dimmed into an inky blackness behind us—darkness into which not even Pharaoh's chariots would dare to venture.

All evening and all night the east wind continued, as the commanders urged our people into formation to begin walking toward the sea. The curtain of darkness hid us completely from the Egyptians' view.

Near dawn, I stood at the head of that grand formation. I looked back over my shoulder at the companies of people as far as my eye could see. The wind was roaring so that my robes were swirling about me and my teeth were gritty with dust. It was no use shouting to Aaron; the wind carried away the sound. Instead, I locked eyes with him and nodded reassurance. His gaze, full of fear and wonder, never left my face. I stretched out my arm toward the sea.　　　　—JB

"It was pointless for me to get lost, even for a second, in any kind of nostalgia for my younger days in Egypt. I had never fit in there, not really. I didn't fit in this camp either, where hostile young men now tried to push past my guards. I had always been too Hebrew for the Egyptians and too Egyptian for the Hebrews.**"**

HIS PLACE IN GOD'S STORY

Although the image that many people now have of Moses is that of a towering leader, it is also important to remember that he harbored feelings of personal inadequacy. Only with the greatest reluctance did he answer God's call to lead the Hebrews. After God called Moses from the burning bush, Moses responded with a series of excuses and objections, some of which may have a familiar ring to us today:

- *"Who am I,* that I should go to Pharaoh and that I should bring out the Israelites from Egypt?" (Exodus 3:11).
- "But look, they will not believe me nor will they heed my voice, for they will say, 'The Lord did not appear to you'" (Exodus 4:1).
- "Please, my Lord, no man of words am I, not at any time in the past nor now since you have spoken to your servant, for I am heavy-mouthed and heavy-tongued" (Exodus 4:10).

The Lord's response to Moses' "Who am I" question is simply, "For I will be with you" (Exodus 4:12). As He does today, the Lord chose as His representative a person who had a combination of flaws and admirable qualities. Moses' success did not depend on his own abilities. Repeatedly, as in the historical fiction above, Moses is put in situations in which only God's intervention can save him. To Moses' credit, he set aside his fears and answered God's call. Will you?

THE STORY FINDS ITS PLACE IN ME

1. What parts of Moses' story find their place in you?

2. This story begins with Moses feeling angry. How much of this anger is justified? Would you be angry in Moses' situation? What does he do with his anger? What can you learn from his response?

3. Examine some of the key commands from the Lord that Moses gives to his people as the Egyptian army bears down on them (Exodus 14:13-14). If you were listening to Moses, how hard do you think it would have been to put these commands into practice? Have you faced battles that only the Lord could fight for you? Have you known times when keeping still was your only option for victory?

4. Instead of choosing Moses to lead His people, God could have chosen someone without Moses' reluctance and excuses, someone more self-assured, with strong speaking skills. Instead, he picked Moses. What can you learn from that about how God may work in your own life? Have you ever felt inadequate for the tasks He has called you to do?

5. God seemed to do things the hard way in Moses' life. How much do you struggle with God's timing and methods in your own life? What may He accomplish in you during times when the journey seems longer than you expected?

NOTES

JOSHUA

THE LEADER • KEY SCRIPTURE PASSAGES: Joshua

HIS CONTEXT

Joshua's story is in many ways the fulfillment of the dream of his ancestor Abraham, his predecessor Moses, and all the generations in between: he and his people finally take the land God has promised, and they settle it. However, they don't take it without a fight. Conquering the land requires many battles, and Joshua captures one territory after another. Then he divides the land among the tribes of Israel, ushering in a new time for the Israelites.

As this new phase of history for the Hebrew people begins, Joshua knows that it is not enough for them to take the *land.* Their spiritual survival also depends on their commitment to the covenant, to serve God only and never stray from Him. As Joshua emphasizes in his remarkable farewell address to the people, they must *choose* whom they will serve. (Joshua 24:14-15, NIV) The people enthusiastically promise that day that they will serve the Lord and will not turn away from Him. We know that their promise is not always kept in the following generations, but Joshua has done what he can to solidify his people's hold on the land and their devotion to God.

HIS STORY

"Clear everyone away!" I order. "Bring me the Warrior."

My advisors, circling me like vultures ready to grab their chunk of flesh, roll their eyes and shift impatiently. "But, Joshua," protests Amihud, their unofficial spokesman, a well-respected but demanding old man, who would push problems at me every hour of the day if I allowed him to, "we have important business to conduct. There's no time for games with this boy—"

"They're not games," I say. "Bring him to me."

It's my favorite time of day, just before dusk, the time when I take an hour or so to set aside the decisions, the complaints, the burdens of leadership to sit outside my tent and look out over the land. This *land* defines my life. We are finally possessing it, this land promised to our ancestor Abraham hundreds of years ago. All of us have spent our lives trying to take hold of the land, but we so rarely take time to *look* at it—the hills in the distance, the bushes and trees, the paths and caves and wild places. Every one of my men would die to defend it, but not one of them wants to sit at sunset and watch the sky turn every shade of red, orange, and purple as the sun sinks beneath the horizon. They are men of action, and I thank God for them, but at dusk I like to sit and marvel at what God has done.

The young man's name is Enan, but I call him Warrior. He is a teenager, barely old enough to be a soldier, but he is hungry for stories of battle. He is eager to fight his own battles, too, more eager than he should be. I have no doubt his appetite for war will be filled before our work is done. He's the son of one of my fiercest fighting men, a man of great courage and sound military advice. At first Enan's father tried to keep his son from bothering me so much, as he pelted me with one question after another, but I told him to leave the boy alone. We need passionate young men who can be taught to carry our commitment to the land and to God's law into the next generation, once old men like me are dead.

Enan strides into the company of his elders with confidence, smiling at me, ignoring the scowls of my advisors who hover at the edge of my little makeshift courtyard. I won't let them come any closer. A fire has been prepared for us. The sun will soon set.

He squats in front of me as if he's preparing for a wrestling match. Our sessions follow a rhythm. He asks me a question, and I ask him a question. Today he

JOSHUA

▼

wastes no time. For just an instant he hesitates and then leans forward, thrusting the question at me like a dagger.

"Sir, today I want to know . . . what have you most feared?"

The men at the edge of the firelight are listening too, I can tell. Enan wants a story about war. That's what he's always after. I've heard his own father tell such stories, barely concealing his bragging under the guise of confessing how terrified he was. Maybe he wants to hear about Jericho again. That's the one everyone talks about. The marching round and round. The blast of the trumpet. The mighty shouts. The walls collapsing at our feet. The staggering victory and the bloody, burning mess we made of that city as we destroyed it.

No war stories today. Today I will surprise him. "I was most afraid of following the great man Moses."

He waits, as if there should be more. Finally he says, "But *you* are the great man, Joshua."

I laugh. Clever boy. Already he knows how to flatter his elders. I tell him, "I was a young man, Enan. A young man like you. How could I possibly follow Moses? He led our people out from bondage under Pharaoh. He brought the Law from the Lord. He persevered against every kind of rebellion, complaint, and disobedience. Who was I to lead in his place?"

"But you *did* step into his place as leader."

"The Lord himself spoke to me, Enan. He said, 'Be strong and courageous.' Four times He repeated it. He wasn't talking about fear of battle or fear of death. He knew I was afraid to lead the people . . . to follow Moses. If I had my way, Moses would have taken us into the land. But we are taking it now. Now let me ask you a question. It may help to answer the one you have asked. *Which is better, the sound of singing or the sound of warfare?*"

I have his attention now, and not only his, but the attention of the growing crowd at the edge of my courtyard. If I had called them all together to make a formal pronouncement, I could not have made them more eager to hear me.

Enan thinks hard before he answers. He suspects a trick question. He probably prefers the sound of warfare, but is that what the great Joshua wants to hear?

Finally he says, "The sound of singing—after the sound of war brings victory."

I laugh. "You are a cunning Warrior. You want *both* answers."

"Am I correct?"

"When I came down with Moses from the holy mountain, as he brought with him the tablets of the covenant, written by God himself, we heard sounds of chaos coming from the camp. It was a sound I had never heard apart from the death cries of battle. 'It is the sound of war!' I told Moses. 'No,' he said as we got closer. 'It is the sound of singing.' He was right, but there was no joy in the song. The people worshiped around the golden calf. Moses smashed the tablets on the ground."

"Don't make that mistake, my Warrior. The victories we have won are not enough. Your generation must *choose* to serve the Lord."

"Yes, son. The war we are fighting is not only on the battlefield. There are many ways to lose it. God has warned us, *Keep the Law burning in your heart*."

"That's how you have led us, sir. You have brought us victory."

I look toward my advisors. This session can't last much longer. Amihud restlessly waits for a moment when he can shoo Warrior away.

"You're young," I say. "You love stories of war. I'm an old man. I have fought many battles, but now I'm full of stories of warning. Many years ago Moses sent me to Canaan to spy out this land that God has given us. It was a land of milk and honey, but the men were afraid to trust God to overcome our enemies. When I begged them not to fear the people in the land, they nearly killed me. God punished them. We all paid the price by having to wait many years longer in that desert. Don't make that mistake, my Warrior. The victories we have won are not enough. Your generation must *choose* to serve the Lord."

Enan looks as if he has another question, but Amihud and the others are already approaching. "I won't forget," the Warrior says, standing, as the old men step forward and all but shove him aside.

I don't hear a word my advisors say as I watch Enan disappear into the darkness toward his tent. I look across the land and feel tired. God has given it, and we have taken it . . . for now. —JB

" The Lord himself spoke to me. He said, 'Be strong and courageous.' Four times He repeated it. He wasn't talking about fear of battle or fear of death. He knew I was afraid to lead the people . . . to follow Moses. If I had my way, Moses would have taken us into the land. But we are taking it now. **"**

HIS PLACE IN GOD'S STORY

It's easy to see why Joshua finds favor both with God and with his mentor and predecessor, Moses. As a young man, Joshua stays steadfast when others fall away. He is not among the revelers who worship the golden calf while Moses is on the mountain with God. When Moses comes down the mountain and he and Joshua approach the camp, the thought of such decadence is so far from Joshua's mind that he thinks he must be hearing the sound of war in the camp rather than the singing and debauchery that are really going on (Exodus 32). Later, when he is one of the twelve men sent to spy out the land promised by God, only he and one other have enough trust in God to urge moving forward despite the dangers (Numbers 13—14).

Joshua's leadership is marked by steadiness, obedience, and sometimes even miracles. The most famous story in which he is involved is the battle of Jericho. Following the Lord's guidance, Joshua orders his fighting men to march around the city, along with seven priests and the ark of the Lord, once a day for six days. Then on the seventh day they march around seven times. At the blast of the trump, they let out a great shout, and the walls of the city crash down. The soldiers attack and achieve a great victory (Joshua 6).

Joshua is heroic as he leads his people in conquering and settling the land God has given them, but he is not perfect. One of the ways in which he fails is that, unlike Moses before him, Joshua does not equip a successor who can lead the people the way he and Moses had. The book of Judges, which follows the book of Joshua, shows the devastating results of this lack of leadership in the next generation. Judges 2:7 says that "the people served the Lord throughout the lifetime of Joshua and of the elders who outlived him and had seen all the great things the Lord had done for Israel" (NIV). However, "After that whole generation had been gathered to their fathers, another generation grew up, who knew neither the Lord nor what he had done for Israel. Then the Israelites did evil in the eyes of the Lord and served the Baals" (Judges 2:10-11, NIV).

THE STORY FINDS ITS PLACE IN ME

1. What parts of Joshua's story find their place in you?

2. One of Joshua's most admirable traits is single-minded devotion to his mission. As the leader of his people, he focuses on securing the land God has given them and solidifying their commitment to God and His Law. He and his people face one obstacle after another, but Joshua keeps bringing his people back to those basics.

What can you learn from that single-mindedness as you consider your own Christian life? What are the basics that you have to cling to no matter what else happens? What can you do to make sure nothing gets in the way of those central priorities?

3. The Lord tells Joshua to "be strong and courageous." He repeats this several times, emphasizing its importance. As you consider your own life, what aspects of it particularly call on strength and courage, as directed by God? What can you do to develop that strength and courage?

4. Read Joshua 22:5. More than anything, Joshua worries most about the people drifting away from God. In what ways is his warning still relevant to us today? Are Christians today in more danger from outside forces or from forces within, such as drifting from the centrality of the gospel message, being lured into false beliefs, and following false "gods"? What can we do as individuals and as a church to combat that drift?

5. What can we learn from Joshua about what makes a good leader?

NOTES

 OTHER STUDIES IN THE NAMED SERIES:

The Unnamed

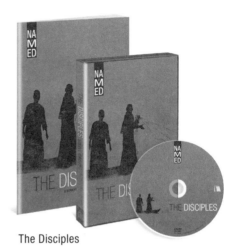

The Disciples

The Women